Rebecca Hood

THE

ENNEAGRAM

The Nine Personality Types.

A Complete Self-Discovery Guide to Spiritual Growth

The Enneagram

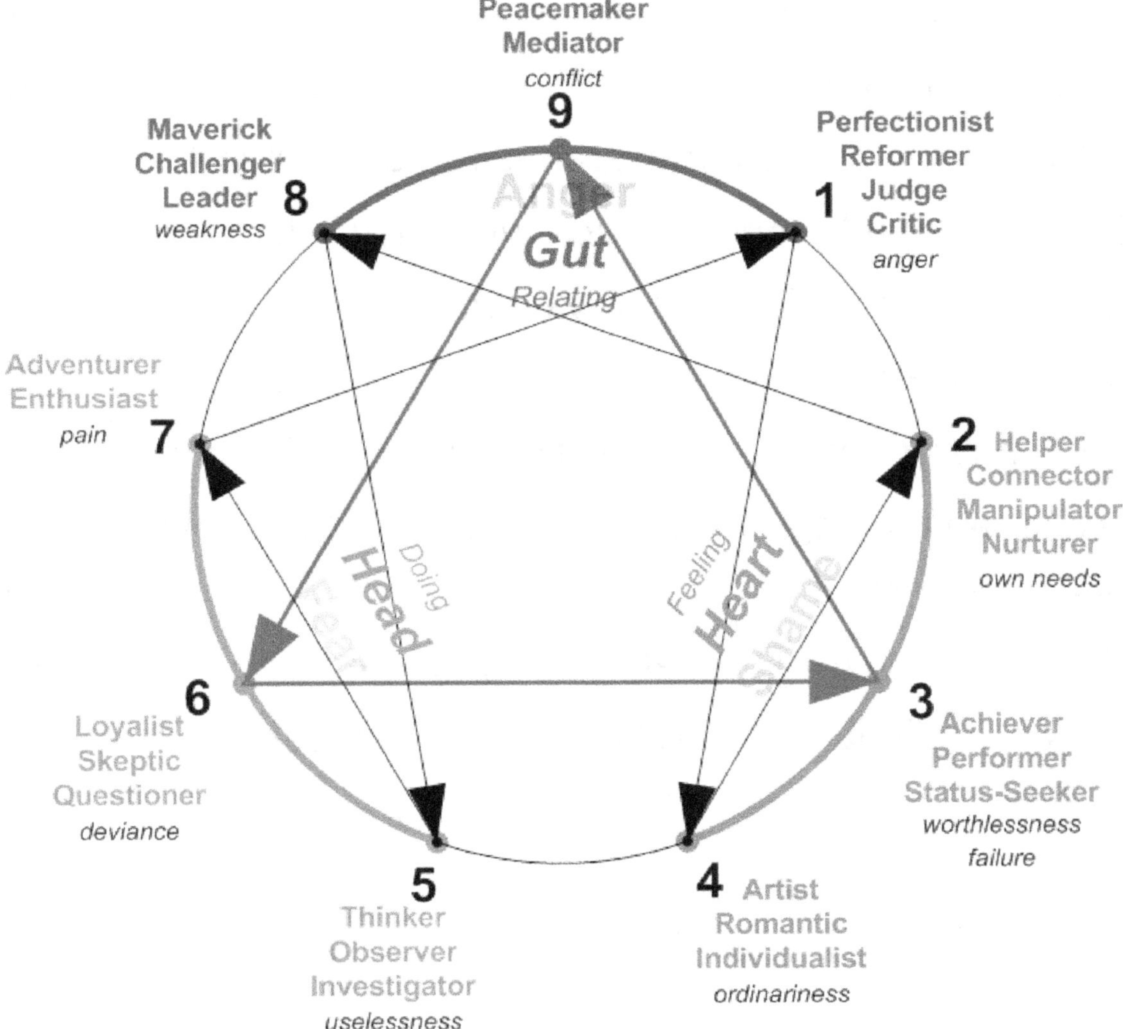

Table of Contents

The Enneagram

The Enneagram is a personality typing system based around nine distinct personality types - the theory being that everyone falls into one of these nine categories. Some say that it is an ancient system with its origins traceable to Sufism, others suggest that it is much more recent. However, it is an interesting system with more complexity than meets the eye at first glance.

Our personality develops in childhood - it is our coping strategy which we develop to deal with our own personal environment. There are nine distinctive patterns recognized in the Enneagram, but it also predicts how each of the nine personalities will change under stress and additionally, when we are feeling completely secure.

So, why would we wish to classify anyone as a specific personality type? Well despite the fact that we can go to the moon, most of us have huge difficulty understanding each other. A key to being able to understand other people is to first develop a proper understanding of ourselves and one way of doing that is to take a look at ourself via the Enneagram.

It is not an easy thing to put your own personality under the microscope. You have to be prepared to hear and discover things about yourself that you may not necessarily want to know. You may not like some of the things you discover. There is no point in finding out something about yourself if you are not prepared to address the findings, and changing your behavior takes time, work and a good deal of commitment.

A couple of points to bear in mind when using the Enneagram: firstly, we need to recognize that all personality types are essentially positive and that any negative behavior you may become aware of can be remedied; secondly, you should be very careful about "typing" someone else i.e. putting somebody into a specific Enneagram category.

Knowing where someone else sits on the 9 points can certainly lead to an improved understanding and better communication. But the downside is that it can also lead to stereotyping people and that might lead you to associate specific negative reactions with certain people. For example, we run the risk of deciding that because somebody is a type 7, this means that they are uncommitted and always will be. Or if someone is a type 9, they will be lazy. By stereotyping people and seeking to predict their reactions, we are imposing our own prejudiced ideas and that's just not a good thing.

As we will see, each of the 9 types of personality has positive and negative characteristics. This makes perfect sense, since no human being is perfect, but it is not healthy to concentrate on the negative aspects of anyone's character. Accepting people for who they are and not what we want them to be leads to improved communication and more enjoyable human relationships.

What does the term Enneagram actually mean?

Broken down, the words Ennea and Gram mean "nine" and "model" respectively. So what are the 9 personality types? The actual names will depend on whichever Enneagram teacher you follow but the underlying classifications are broadly the same:

The Perfectionist/Reformer

The Giver/Helper

The Performer/Achiever

The Tragic Romantic

The Observer

The Trooper

Dreamer/the Epicure

Confronter/the Boss

Peacemaker/Mediator

By knowing your own type, you can become much more understanding of other people's reactions. Motivating yourself to achieve things in life will become easier if you understand the drivers for your own behaviour. Followers of the Enneagram believe that everyone has one primary underlying motivational driver that, to a large extent, determines our thoughts, feelings and actions.

This underlying driver or passion creates a person's paradigm or view of life. The passion is given a negative name but it does not mean that the personality type is negative. It means that the personality is primarily addicted to that specific behavior. But this is the raw material - with work, self examination and understanding, all personality types are capable of turning this "negative" into a positive.

For example, type 2, the giver, believes that everyone needs help. The underlying motivation is pride. The type 2 personality takes pride in believing that it can help everyone thus developing an inflated sense of self worth. But by examining and understanding this motivation in life, it can convert this pride to humility and use its natural gift for helping people in a better way.

The underlying driver for type 9 is sloth i.e. being lazy about life. Making decisions takes energy since they must weigh up both sides of the argument, so it is easier just to ignore difficulties and wait for them to go away or for someone else to resolve them. Nines value harmony above everything else. If an understanding of this driver is not developed, they will spend their lives trying to avoid conflict or side stepping arguments.

But Nines, like all the other personality types, can be a fantastic asset to the world. Once they understand that their basic underlying motivation is sloth, they can improve by setting small goals and structuring processes to ensure that they achieve them. Their natural wish to avoid conflict allows them to develop emotional detachment which is very useful in volatile situations.

It is very important to realize that everyone has only one type - you cannot be a member of two camps! Some people, especially those that have just started studying the Enneagram, think that they are a mixture of the different personality types. They identify characteristics which appear to support this theory. Our personal characteristics are not the same as our underlying motivation. We can have similar characteristics and reactions to other people and yet be totally different personality types.

It may be difficult to classify yourself as a particular type. We all have an image of who we are rather than knowledge of who we are. It might be useful to ask a very close friend, whom you trust 100%, to give you some feedback on your personality. Be careful though; not all friendships can survive this type of honesty! And remember that each personality type has positive and negative aspects associated with it. Don't get hung up about the negatives. Instead, pour all your energy into developing the positive aspects of your character.

The Spread of Enneagram and Understanding its Basics

Enneagram is essentially a geometric number that followers of Pythagoras, the great mathematician, have been using for over 2,500 years. It managed to spread throughout the world thanks to such great civilizations as Babylon and Greece, which adopted this system of thinking.

It consists of a total of nine points located in a circle. Each of these points is clearly defined and labeled using numbers from one to nine. Numbers are used to indicate this personality, can be verified by the Enneagram laboratory. However, no personality is better than the other. Therefore, a person whose personality is, first of all, not inferior to a person who is in ninth place.

Wondering what these nine points, in fact, presents; these personality traits and its nine basic features, which include the personality of every person on Earth. Each of these points is connected to two other points using the interconnection lines, forming a type of stellar characters.

When you participate in Enneagram labs, you will be able to determine which point represents your personality. But it's not good to know. However, the main catch of this technique is the lines connecting different points. When you're angry, you move in with another person, whereas when you're happy, you're a completely different person. Therefore, using these lines and arrows marked on them, you can easily determine the course that they are ghosts, to take in the event of stress or joy.

Therefore, knowing what will pass, a coach could help you to refrain from the bad personality; each has a drawback, but it is usually the ugliest part of your life.

It's not just the numbers and lines that make up the Enneagram diagram. In addition to these factors, there are also wings. The wings are placed in such a way that they refer to two numbers located near the numbers of your type of personality. Most people have the characteristics of one of these wings and very rarely both.

These nine personalities are classified to fall into three triads: the idea of a trained personality, personality, sensitivity and finally, the personality based on instinct. Just think about yourself, you will definitely fall into one of these categories, and therefore you will also find a place in the nine.

Is it about the structure of the Enneagram, but if you want to control your personality type, you'll need to find someone who is a computer expert, or you could attend Enneagram workshops, as well as many other participants.

Guide to the Enneagram of Personality

So, you are an absolute beginner in Enneagram... You've heard how amazing and useful this can be, but you're not sure what it is... Well, if you want to get the absolute basis of the Enneagram, then sit down and read.

Before continuing, I want to remind you that there are a number of different ways to interpret what we know about Enneagram. There are several "school of Thought" on the subject that will undoubtedly learn more than you delve into the subject. What you are about to read, is stolid, stubborn, only partially informed, but, hopefully, just to give you Enneagram taste. Most importantly, it pushes you deeper.

Enneagram is literally a symbol. It is a nine-pointed symbol that has appeared in many religions over the past millennia. No one knows for sure how the ancients invented the study or how they used it until recently. Enneagram spectre sums up speculation about the origin of the Enneagram in this way:

"The Roots Of The Enneagram are questionable. Some authors believe that they found variations of the symbol of the Enneagram in the Sacred Geometry of Pythagoras, who, 4000 years ago, was interested in the deep meaning and meaning of numbers. This line of mystical mathematics was adopted by Plato, his disciple Plotinus, and the following neo-Platonists.

Some believe that this tradition found its way into esoteric Judaism through Philo, a neo-Platonic Jewish philosopher, where it later appears as the tree of life, Cabalistic symbolism ninefold ness.

Variants of this symbol also appear in the Islamic traditions of the Sufi, perhaps they come through the Arab philosopher al-Ghazzali. Around the Fourteenth Century order Naqshbandi Sufism, variously known as "the Brotherhood of bees" (because they collected and stored knowledge) and "Symbolists" (because they taught through symbols) is said to have been preserved and transmitted to the symbol of the Enneagram.

Speculation is the Enneagram found its way into esoteric Christianity by Pseudo-Dionysius (which was influenced by the neo-Platonist), and mystic Ramon Lull (which was influenced by his Islamic studies.)

On the facade of the textbook written in the seventeenth century by the Jesuit mathematician student Athanasius Kircher, a number similar to the Enneagram appears."

In recent years, Enneagram "rediscovered" Oscar Ichazo, a Chilean philosopher who taught at the Arica Institute in Chile. Ichazo, I think, was the first to actually apply the laws of the Enneagram nine laws that in the human psyche.

As the Enneagram is understood today, it is a tool that will help you understand and formulate nine "filters" that anyone can use to see the world. These filters are fluid, intangible, which may or may not actually exist, but using them as tools can cause drastic realization in relationships or in your personal growth.

I think comparing these filters as the "operating systems" of a computer is a great way to understand it. Some people are Windows, some people run Linux, and some people use Apple computers. It's just another way to take sensory input, organize it, and react.

The beauty of this study is that if you can express the deepest feelings and ideas of your friends, loved ones, and especially yourself, you can get a perspective that was not there before. You see clearly. Like never before...

Different schools have Enneagram in many different directions. Some offer advice on how to achieve professional success, some offer it for life coaches help their clients with information. Some will move you to the limit, find places in your personality that you can use pictures. And many schools do many other things that are beyond the realm of control of this absolute beginner. I'm here to discover, use and report.

I would like to remind you that this is only the shortest exam. There is much more to understand and live before starting to reap the fruits of the Enneagram. But I can assure you that with enough time and energy, and self-awareness is the Enneagram on the path to peace and satisfaction stronger than anything I have ever discovered.

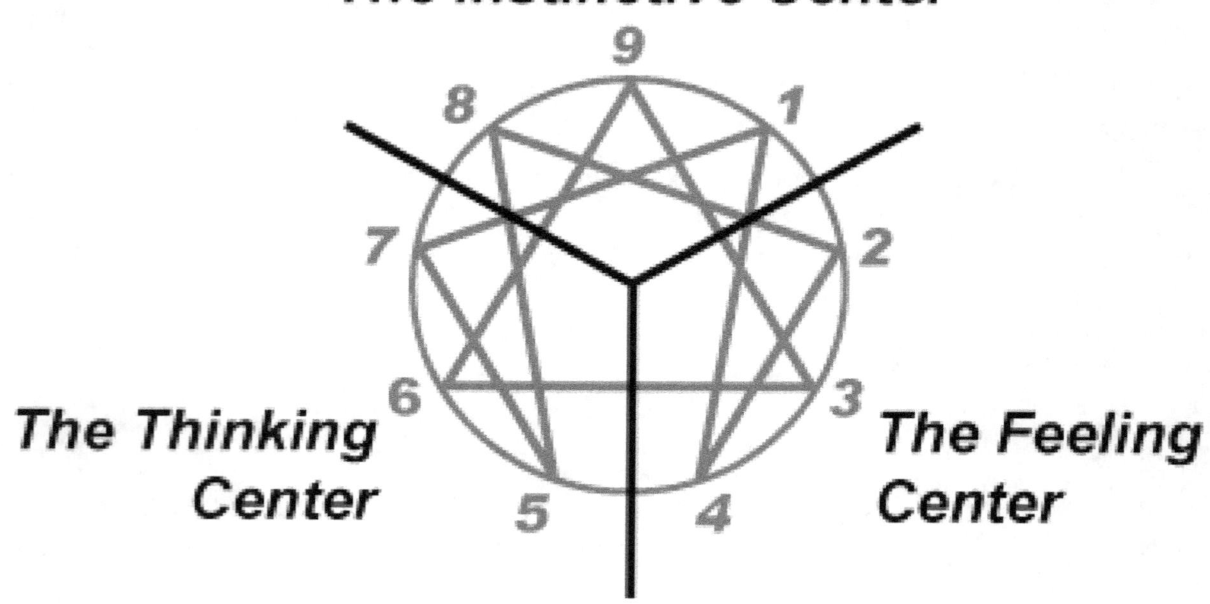

The Instinctive Center
9
8
1
7
2
6
3
5
4
The Thinking
Center
The Feeling
Center

Introduction to The Enneagram of Personalities

The Enneagram has been around for many centuries in various forms, what I have in mind in this article is most often called the Enneagram of personality, and is a combination of ancient wisdom and modern psychology. The word Enneagram means "9-pointed star" and refers to the traditional representation of Enneagram in schematic form.

9 points refers to a way of seeing the world we live in: how we relate to it and how it worries us. Nine ways to see the world are strategies that each of us must respond to situations where we are stressed or relaxed. In life we tend to adopt one of these strategies above all others, which has implications for how we behave in other circumstances.

A useful analogy to explain what an Enneagram is and what it does is a comparison between people with a computer. The computer has hardware, software and memory; its core is an operating system, without which the computer can not function.

Operating system: Windows XP / Windows Vista / MAC / Linux / other

Material: computer case, CD, hard drive, etc.

Program

CPU: central processor unit that performs all calculations on the computer

Memory: RAM memory

The Software enables the computer to perform specific tasks, and memory (RAM), as well as the central processing unit decides how fast it can do.

We are accustomed every few years to update the computer operating system, taking into account the latest developments in computer technology. So many of us use the latest version of Windows now. We know that if we try to use the latest software with the old operating system, the software will not work the way it was designed or not work at all. We also know that the more we try to run programs at the same time, the more memory we use, and the computer will be slower, sometimes even crashes.

In the human body, we also have a similar configuration:

Operating system: one of nine Enneagram models

Material: our body

Software: skills we learned in life

Memory: brain

However, unlike a computer, most of us never updated the operating system takes account of recent developments (learning from our life); in fact, most of them have no idea about which operating system is installed in the first place!

Start the operating system, which in most cases has been fully installed for two years, and certainly no later than at the age of five years, we strive to use the latest software on it. Then we wonder why these abilities cannot give a result, they (new software applied to the old operating system). In addition, we have a number of unsolved questions of life(open Program Files), which are increasingly using our CPU and memory; so we slow down, as life goes on, and some of us even collapse (nervous breakdown).

This is a very simplified analogy with the computer, but it well explains the role of Enneagram models in our lives. Like on a computer, there is nothing we can do without an operating system. And just like on a computer, this operating system limits what we can do according to the rules / limits of the same operating system.

How does that help you?

Enneagram is the way out of this circle of limitations. It provides us with knowledge of the main operating system, which controls all of our actions and allowing us to modernize this system, then we will start working to its full potential. How can we solve the problems of our lives if we do not know what causes this problem?

The Enneagram Model turned out to be very powerful, not only in mapping human behavior, but also in the processes of sustainable personal development and transformation. It has been used throughout its history to allow people to exceed the limits of their operating system.

Make it a specific goal to follow the task, from start to finish.

Remember that having several projects at once can be a way to try to escape reality.

Stop thinking that anyone who disagrees with you is criticizing you. Constructive criticism is often useful.

If you are dealing with flames, or you live in fantasy, embrace your real life and find reasons to be optimistic and radiate good mood in life.

The Enneagram Personality Types

THE PERFECTIONIST/REFORMER

These are people who need to do things. Perfectionists are usually critical, idealistic and critical. Decisions are made in the knowledge of "the only correct way."Their work should reflect extremely strict standards set by themselves. They constantly teach, preach and control others. Through this, others feel chosen or rejected. Perfectionist, the fiercest anger is directed to itself. At best, perfectionists are honest, idealistic, and visionary. They have a clear vision of what it should be, with the ability to drive others.

This type of personality is also called a reformer. Their basic motivation is anger. Aim for perfection in life and when it does not happen, often angry and very anxious. These are extremely loyal people with high moral values, who try very hard to protect and take care of your family and loved ones.

They have many features. They have an excellent view for details, for example. In fact, they dot all the letters "I "and cross all the letters" T "in everything they do. Guided by a strict internal criticism is always very difficult to ensure that all they do was what is most perfect. This increases their need for improvement, which can be beneficial for all parties involved, but it can also prove burdensome for both 1. Type and people to whom Type 1 reform efforts.

But they also have negative qualities. They can very quickly judge others, even if they feel very guilty. Despite their obvious gifts, often do not appreciate their own worth and tend to fight with their inner criticism - the voice in my head, telling them how useless they are. They tend to believe that others are simply nice when they give them extra.

Because they are perfectionists, they put themselves under constant pressure to improve, work harder and get more. Thanks to this, they can appear optimistic and indifferent in Group situations.

Are you a perfectionist?

Do you have a strong inner voice that constantly criticizes you?

Do you often wonder how you could have done something better or faster?

Do you have a problem accepting compliments for your work?

Want to make it easier for you?

Do you do the work of others because they do not meet your standards?

The other perfectionists call you?

If you have identified yourself as a perfectionist, try these simple tips that will help you restore one of the positive aspects of your personality type:

Learn to accept a compliment and believe in his sincerity.

Learn to relax more

You have to take time to have fun.

Find a way to silence your inner critic.

Recycle your thoughts to be more positive

Work on the most negative characteristics of your personality type: a tendency to get angry with others, a tendency to judge and the belief that it is your role to straighten the world out regardless of the consequences.

Having studied and evaluated yourself, you can learn to deal with these negatives so that your personality is glued to the positive qualities of your type. The hard work, which leads when needed and trying to change the world for the sake of others are your positive characteristics, and these will naturally be highlighted when you learn to control the negatives.

THE HELPER

The aid must be assessed. They give with the intention of mutual recognition. Helpers focus on the relationship with an emotionally seductive approach. Kind and manipulative, helpers become indispensable and adore others. This is their way of influencing and seeking power. Assistants have an impeccable radar for other feelings, preferences and appetites. They excel in customer service, they are really sensitive and modest. Helpers serve and bring the best in others.

Helpers want to help the world and his mother. They tend to solve everyone's problems because they think they can solve them. Their main motivation is Pride: everyone who tends to think needs help.

Their feature is that they are extremely kind and help their neighbors. They are big supporters and right-wing people because they basically like to be a help provider. The well-being of the individual is the most important thing.

The personality type of the donor does not tend to be a good leader. In general, they do not like goals and are not primarily task-oriented. They can leave you too emotionally involved, which can often lead to negative feelings like the impression that they are being used. These negative feelings can sometimes cause a lack of objectivity and can easily lose sight of their role.

Helpers are generally spared from having to deal with their own needs and problems, because they are too busy helping others. Often they can be the wrong decision-makers, because they often lack the overall picture - the needs of the individual, which helps at some point is decisive, as far as they are concerned.

Are you a helper?

You don't like doing certain tasks that you have to do because you don't see the point in them?

Are you the happiest when you help others achieve their goals or solve their problems?

Do you often feel taken for granted that people have helped you not to thank enough?

Do you think you often start projects, but don't you see them through the way you distract yourself from others and their problems?

If you have identified yourself as an assistant, try these simple tips that will help you restore the positive aspects of your personality type:

Identify your needs and spend time to meet them. Make a journal note if necessary, you can say that you can not help x, Y or z until you have done at least one thing on your list to help you.

Begin to believe that you are not responsible for everyone and can not solve all problems.

Get better identification when people really need your help, and when they are better left alone to resolve themselves.

You can change your tendency to seek the approval of others and its tendency to desire attention in more positive qualities of compassion and focus on other human beings. This will help you build a long-term friendship, which will help you fulfill your basic motivation to feel needed in a much more positive way.

THE PRODUCER

Producers are more than likely workaholics. They like to be applauded for doing their job. Manufacturers can be very successful, enthusiastic and competitive. It is necessary that they be rewarded for their achievements. Some might say that producers are involved and obsessed with the image. They are distinguished as insensitive, superficial, artificial and timely. Manufacturers are often considered their resume. Manufacturers, at best, are impatient and effective leaders with the ability to solve problems and influence others.

Expert

It is easy for a connoisseur to gravitate to the beautiful, authentic, true and unusual. These people are romantic and melancholy. Connoisseurs show perfect taste in their fears. They're looking for a deeper meaning below the surface. The feelings that drive their decision. It seems that connoisseurs are satisfied with the impeccable. They may seem intense or arrogant. At best, they are creative and imaginable. Connoisseurs like the attractiveness, taste and elegance of the world.

Wise

The sages try to dominate their personal domains. They are emotionally distant. They say a wise view of the world from certain points of view. Here they can store facts, theories and information. Trials are not based on relationships, but mask and minimize needs. Others see him emotionally separated, as they hide behind what they find. The tests are at best sensitive, insightful, respectful, intense, enterprising. Engagement and most wizards in their fields.

Usefulness of Problem Solving

At best, paranoid grocery stores fear worst-case scenarios. Trust is a big problem. They are over-prepared and obsessed with what might go wrong. For others, postponing them can be frustrating. Grocery stores can be faithful, imaginative, original thinkers, intuitive, determined, sensitive and courageous. They are known to defend their team, their boss and themselves. Grocery stores are great for reporting traps and patterns hidden along the way.

Visionary

Visionaries remain positive and keep all options open. They engage, plan and have high-energy novels. Visionaries have a hard time growing up. They are known as the shallow Peter Pans. It is not easy for fortune tellers to think about traps. Therefore, they avoid completion, pain, conflicts, ordinary commitments and routine work. Even if they begin to progress, they often neglect them. The best visionaries are gifted, spiritual, inspiring and charming. Their thoughts and enthusiasm attract people.

The superior Dog

Power and control are what the best dogs are looking for. They express their feelings freely and loudly. Upper dogs are described as dominant and blunt. They are loudly looking for clashes with the belief that the truth often comes out in battle. They focus on their own capabilities and other shortcomings. Others may be discouraged by their fiery intimidation. At best, dogs should have strangers to whom they command.

Mediators try to include all people and all opinions. These people are easily compromised. He sees the feelings, needs and passions of others. Others may perceive mediators as negligent or decomposed. At best, mediators lead the inspiration of others. They are warm and open individuals. Intermediaries are naturally in contact with the flow of the group. The mediators are therefore excellent diplomats, team builders and Border keepers.

THE PERFORMER

Interpreters are freelancers who tend to nurture a deep fear of failure. They often measure success based on the respect and consent they receive from others.

This is an image orientated people who can provide externally positive and well groomed appearance despite the sometimes completely desperate and negative feeling his life.

They're great politicians because they instinctively know when to keep quiet. Also excel in sales and advertising roles, that their positivity and go attitude tends to attract other people.

Their positive qualities can make a great leader, but when the pursuit of success can sometimes cause resentment and frustration. They rely on their natural charisma and charm to get them out of these difficulties of sticky personal relationships. They are natural speakers and are so optimistic and confident that they believe they could probably sell snow to the Eskimos.

The disadvantage of their personality type is that they do not suffer any criticism, even if it means constructively. They often interpret criticism as a failure. As masters of communication, they can easily use sarcasm as a way to sink someone else. Since their main motivation is fear of failure, will be intolerant to any socially unacceptable behavior. This can relate to improper behavior at the table, rudeness or boldness of their children. Anything that might potentially reflect poorly on them is simply not tolerated.

Are you an artist?

Do you often feel like wearing a mask or playing a role? The world sees confident, go getter, while you can see someone who is a bit of a failure?

Do you have very few close friends, but many friendly acquaintances are mainly related to your field of work?

Is it hard for you to relax and do nothing?

Are you afraid of letting people come near you in case they see you "failed"?

Are you worried that other people you work with will eventually find out you're not capable of doing something right?

Try these simple tips to help you recover the positive aspects of your personality type if you are a succeeder:

Allowing other people to love what's real is not your job or your financial situation.

Learn to accept yourself-get rid of the mask. Although no one likes serial moans, people who are always at the top of the world can be hard to live with

Try to enjoy your life as it is currently. Stop waiting for another pay rise or promotion.

You can learn how to channel your negative feature of hectic activity into your destination settings.

Instead of focusing on external success, use your natural skills to work for the benefit of everyone's success.

THE TRAGIC ROMANCE

They tend to see their lives as some kind of tragedy. They tend to constantly live in the past and feel that life has somehow overcome them. Basically, they feel that something is missing, because they do not seem to accept the banality of their everyday life. However, they tend to be in the spotlight.

Romantic-in the sense of the Romantic movement in the arts (wild, Byronic) is also known as the individualist, they have clear values and standards and tend to be very sensitive. If this sensitivity is used positively, they are sensitive and penetrating people, they realize the needs and desires of their neighbors. They have very loyal friends and show great sympathy for others. They are great teachers because they have the ability to inspire others, even to greatness.

But when used negatively, this sensitivity results in very tense and sensitive people with whom it can be very difficult to live. They can be ready to delegate responsibility for everything, including their own life, as they easily get bored with "normal" things. They want a "romantic dream", but often lose interest when it really becomes available.

Past relationships become more "perfect" over time, and current relationships fade in comparison with them. They don't see that their current life would be fun if they accepted what they had.

Some questions to ask if you think you can be this:

Are you stuck in the past exploring relationships that might be?

Do you gravitate to the dramatic side of life: clothes, food and people?

Do you often experience so many different emotions that you are not sure what you feel and become overwhelmed?

Do you suffer from a feeling of loss or abandonment, even if you are in a close relationship?

Tips that try to minimize downsides include:

The pain of a past relationship, but make sure you let it go. Stop rebuilding and rediscovering the past.

Work to reduce dramatic crises and learn to control your mood swings.

Recognize the merits of your current life and your partner.

Use your sensitivity to help others cope with their pain while building a support network, which will comfort you when you need it.

You can minimize your introspective behavior, and feelings of discouragement and focus on loving yourself and using your natural abilities to show compassion and help others.

THE OBSERVER

As the name suggests, this type of personality traces the world from the safety of their ivory tower. Their goal is to achieve greater clarity and understanding of the world around them. They do not like confrontation or dissent, so they tend to take the opinion of a third party, refuse to be involved in any family quarrel.

They tend to create stubborn leaders, because they are fully confident in their capabilities. They "knew" that they would already have a deeper understanding of the topic or otherwise have the opportunity to learn it. Observers, like decisions in the workplace, because they believe in logical thinking, but transfer responsibility for emotional decision, i.e. to those who are engaged in relation to the other side.

The positive aspects of this type of personality are their curiosity in people and the world around them, and that makes them willing to try new ideas. They have great courage and do not tend to judge other human beings. Encourage others to develop their own independence, because they are happy to delegate and trust others in your team.

Negative behavior with this type of personality is, as with other types, a violation of their strengths. Because they are by nature analytical, he believes that everyone has his own life under control, so he can be completely motionless. They do not believe in fate, so any misfortune that you can suffer depends on your incompetence.

Observers tend to be very bad at asking for help, because they believe they already know everything they need to know or have the ability to find out. This makes them very enterprising people, but they can also be difficult for others to live.

Are you an observer? Try these questions:

Are you thirsty for knowledge and information?

Do you find the lack of logical thinking of other people extremely annoying?

Waiting for something new, unexpected and quickly bored by repetition?

A few simple tips to help strengthen the positive side of this type of personality:

Learn to assess spontaneity-not everything needs to be planned to the smallest detail.

Believe in your freedom to express your emotions.

It's okay to ask for help - you can not know everything.

Instead of being selfish and uncompromising, you know the world around you and freely use your knowledge to help others.

SOLDIER / GUARDIAN

The soldier is also known as the guardian of teachers involved in Enneagram. This type of personality always tries to avoid danger. Their basic motivation is a deep lack of confidence, so look for groups with well-defined values.

The positive side of this type of personality is that they make great friends and companions. They are loyal, courageous and utterly devoted to their group of friends. Sincerely care about others and are working to make the world a better place for all to enjoy. Warmth and natural affection as a good sense of humor. They value the state and they work very hard to achieve that.

Aware of where there is danger in the environment, there are six phobic and anti-phobic. Six phobics tend to avoid danger, while six counterphobics realize danger, but also ready to face it head on. In what could be considered a dangerous profession, there are a high number of six counterproductive phobias.

Since this type of personality lacks self-confidence, they can have a blinding faith in authority. They will follow the figure of authority independently and take the position "they will know better". When asked to spontaneously contribute to the decision-making process, they are often undecided and speak reluctantly, while questioning what they say. They often worry, are anxious and concerned and need to feel that they are integrating into their group.

Do you match this type of personality? Try these questions:

Do you like to entertain people in the comfort of your home?

Do you prefer a day full of activity and do not like leisure, that you are not sure how to spend it?

Do you think it's hard to make decisions, preferring that others do for you?

You prefer an authoritarian boss, who sets very strict rules to adhere to rather than a more relaxed boss, who likes to delegate responsibility and make the decision for you?

If you get into this type of personality, try these tips:

Avoid postponement by setting deadlines for achieving specific objectives.

Do not avoid the task simply because the instructions are confusing-ask for an explanation instead.

Look for feedback from a group of trusted friends and family so you can solve your self-confidence issues.

Having a strong conscience and being faithful to others is better than being defenseless and insecure about yourself.

INTERMEDIATE / PEACEMAKER

This type of personality wants to create harmony between them and the rest of the world. They suppress their emotions for fear of moving the boat. He believes that you should not make waves-you can not please everyone, so why bother to try at all. Their basic motivation is laziness. They can be inventive and tend to use common sense to solve problems or problems they encounter. You've probably heard someone who was described as a "sweet giant" - that would be the perfect description for that type of personality.

Once they master their personality type, the positive elements of inner peace and tranquility make them specialists in treating difficult people. It is balanced, they do not have a lure, and therefore their presence has a calming effect on the most volatile situations. They are able to maintain a healthy separation, thereby preventing the need to take sides in the argument. For this reason, they are good referees.

However, mediators may suffer from a lack of self-esteem that forces them to deal with the past. They do not appreciate themselves or their entry into relationships, which helps them to justify their basic motivation of laziness. Their display is: my opinion is not so important, so why waste time and energy, put it on.

In the world of work, although very capable in their work, they often avoid being promoted to positions that involve stress and responsibility. If they are in conflict to avoid at all costs, they will often ignore even a direct question, if they know the answer, someone gets angry. They will remain silent until the other side solves the problem or gives up the effort. By imposing silence, they do not need to provoke conflicts or face the consequences.

If you are an intermediary?

Do people comment on the fact that you will do anything to avoid a fight even if you leave if necessary?

Work on the basis that if you keep your thoughts to yourself, you can not cause an argument?

Do people see you as an easy way when you are inside a riot?

Do you prefer simple joys in life?

A few tips to help your qualities shine through:

Try to set personal goals and set the deadlines in which they must be achieved.

Learn to know what you want, not what others want.

Using small steps, try to make a decision.

When someone asks you something, think about what you want and admit it rather than keep quiet.

Stop doubting yourself and learn to accept and make love. You have the ability to move mountains once you maximize the positive aspects of your personality.

THE DREAMER / EPICURE

He believes that the world is full of opportunities, and therefore spends all his time and energy searching for ways to facilitate life. They are very intuitive people with high levels of energy and have trouble relaxing because they are so biased, that match the pieces of the puzzle of life.

Their motivation is the fear of discomfort or pain, and they make great efforts not to experience these feelings. They're compulsive optimists. There is a solution to every problem: you just need to find it.

From a positive point of view is of 7 types of often visionary and idealistic, who may have the means to solve our global problems. He believes everyone is good at heart, even if it takes a car to dig deep enough to find him. Trust your peers tend to highlight the best in people. They are ideal entrepreneurs, because they do not believe in failure and change tactics if necessary.

But Dreamers often difficult to see the project to the end, how to focus on Joy and grind their teeth, and often the result is not very funny. The most successful usually uses a different type of personality to perform tasks such as recognizing their weakness. Dreamers crave the pleasure they get by pursuing new challenges. This type of personality is associated with the "mortal" sin of the throat, as it stimulates its dependence on pleasure from anything else.

So, are you fit for the role of Dreamer?

Do you immediately start looking for a solution when the problem is presented to them, even if it belongs to someone else?

Can you talk to someone? Are people looking for dinners and other social events? Were you the most popular boy in school?

People often comment on how "gifted" you are?

Tips for treating the negative side of the Dreamer type:

They make it a specific goal to follow the task, from start to finish.

Remember that having several projects at once can be a way to try to escape reality.

Stop thinking that anyone who disagrees with you is criticizing you. Constructive criticism is often useful.

If you are dealing in the flames, or you live in fantasy, embrace your real life and find reasons to be optimistic and radiate good mood in life.

Lead by consensus.
Lead by strategy and big action.
Lead by example and standard setting.
Lead by new ideas and innovation.
Lead by motivation and encouragement.
Lead by creative problem solving.
Lead by goals, plans and results.
Lead by research, deliberation and planning.
Lead by vision and connection.
9
8
1
7
2
6
3
5
4

Introduction to the Enneagram as a Leadership Tool

The Enneagram is a fascinating tool of nine orientations that allows us to get a deep vision of our true potential. Try to give us an overview of how we fund our basic assumptions that worked for us or not! (It somehow provides a generic manual for life! The little book we all hoped for came with us to provide us with insightful advice on how we recruit and treat with care.)

Leadership development requires fluidity at this level. Margaret Jackson, CEO of Qantas, said: "Know Yourself, respect others, be brave and brave."This tool allows you to make the first two to a depth rarely available in psychological profiling. From this basis, with the wisdom of recognition, the next two become natural behaviors.

The Enneagram was founded in the oral tradition until recently, so its origin is unclear. Some argue that there is evidence of its use in the Babylonian era, others are currently in court to discuss their rights to its use.

Some use it as a personality tool I prefer as a roadmap, a generic blue for your "model" of assumptions that can be used to direct intentional and targeted growth. It allows you to eradicate assumptions that go beyond their use by date, perhaps formulated in childhood, and the growth of wiser concepts.

Application

The Enneagram of orientation of the individual is determined partly objectively, knowing their assumptions, and partly subjectively, finding the reason for their actions.

As such, it fits perfectly into the most recent assumptions of quantum physics only by measuring the events we can influence (there is a subjective component to each observation). Our language has lagged behind these Terms and we still prefer the objectivity provided, which is more true. However, the information provided by the interview and the convenience of working with others have always been the final test for compatibility rather than the psychological tools of screening.

Questionnaires for determining our orientation in the program, which are easily available on the web, is not very accurate. Not because of the skill of the questionnaire compiler, but because of the inability to objectively assess our subconscious motive and compare it with others. How many thoughts have you ever had about this area of your life?

When I work with Enneagram for 15 years, I still consider it, despite strict tests. A qualified specialist can provide information to identify the orientation of the person or, if necessary, those who know us well.

The most eloquent ideas in our orientation are those that are based on the behavior of a person in conflict. Because we assume that our conflict is well dressed, we do it with abandonment - with each other we are the emperor without clothes and often perceive our actions with great clarity. Consult an experienced general practitioner or ask your relatives, colleagues or friends to help you identify your orientation.

Leadership Development

Much of the literature informs us that we can create ourselves to be leaders, we must not be born this way. However, there is little in the literature that will direct us to fertile ground so that we can develop our leadership and our abilities.

Enneagram shows us our holes (limits) and our mountains (talents). Our task as a leader is to develop conscious skills with both! Enneagram shows us where they are so we can start working our lives.

Creating Leadership with the Enneagram

Many of you will know that you are passionate about how the Enneagram creates extraordinary self-awareness as a way to change your life and work in an infinite positive way.

This is an incredibly dynamic and deep profile beyond personality, showing how your life orientation affects your happiness, success, efficiency, how others perceive you. It shows you how you can move to its full potential, as well as how you can sabotage and brake.

Currently, I use the Enneagram in their executive coaching (individuals and teams) to help them understand and maximize their individual leadership style and the style of their colleagues. Last November, I did an advanced course (nine areas) with the Enneagram Institute in New York on using Enneagram to develop teams to their full potential.

Knowing how your individual Enneagram type creates your signature leadership style, and the potential (as well as pitfalls) individual and person approach is not only enlightening, but it is actually essential to create your own authentic way of leading your team and organization.

Here are some quick examples of leadership opportunities and pitfalls by type:

Type 1: idealist or reformer

+ 1 types are truly visionary, idealistic, passionate about their individual leadership roles and corporate mission. As such, they can inspire their team to new levels of success, determination and enthusiasm.

- With their high standards and idealism, type 1 can be painfully self-critical and demanding of yourself, others, who drive. This can be demotivating and unproductive, and their direct relationships and colleagues sometimes consider type 1 to be too hard and rigorous master tasks.

Type 2: Assistant or caregiver

+ Type 2s lead with heart and inspire your team and their ability to connect emotionally and empathy.

- Type 2 can be too emotional, become particularly sensitive to derailment if their personal or professional relationships break; sometimes they can resort to emotional blackmail, if they feel destitute, which clearly compromises effective leadership.

Type 3: The Achiever

+ Type 3s are passionately trained in Excel and many successful leaders are in this type. Their commitment to success (sometimes almost at any cost) often provides excellent results and the accompanying commitment of his team.

- Sometimes the 3 are so obsessed that they will do everything necessary to ensure "success" at all costs, which leads to inauthentic leadership, where the 3 burn themselves and their teams, lose the connection with priorities and values.

Type 4: Individual / Creative

+ 4 types are often persuasive, charismatic, creative and inspired by deep thinkers, inspiring their teams to excel in the same way, using their own individual values and strengths

- The 4 can sometimes derail when they don't feel valued, or if they feel they don't have enough space to use their individual leadership style and their gifts shine. When this happens, they may appear as too individualistic, not team players, too dramatic and intense.

Type 5: Thinker

+ Type 5s can be brilliant, original, visionary and profound leaders, able to create extraordinary results with their analytical and creative thinking.

- Type 5s can become isolated leader, lose the ability to connect with and inspire your team, it comes cold and too lonely.

Type 6: The Loyalist

+ Type 6s are engaging, dedicated and hardworking leaders who inspire their similar teams, often using humor as effective strategies

- If you are under stress, 6 leaders derail anxiety and negativity, so they focus on the worst scenarios, which will lose the confidence of your team, sometimes leads to low morale, even panic.

Type 7: Passionate

+ Type 7 are enthusiastic, charming and fun leaders who can inspire their teams with the strength of their personality and energy

-7 leaders can lose concentration, dissipate and lose connection to their own emotional authenticity, thus undermining their team and weakening collective concentration and performance

<u>**Type 8: The Challenger**</u>

+ Type 8s are powerful, charismatic, strong and natural leaders who naturally command the trust and loyalty of their team

- 8S can deteriorate in bullying behavior as leaders, causing their team to be bullied by, even scared and alienated

<u>**Type 9 s: The Peacemaker**</u>

+ Type 9 s are common, harmonious, "We" leaders, experienced people to work together effectively to create innovative results

Nines can become too collaborative, not pushing hard enough, not pushing forward and losing the confidence of their team.

Do you know your type of Enneagram? If so, why not think about these points and consider how to maximize your authentic leadership by working with the awareness of your Enneagram type?

Interpersonal Communication with the Enneagram

Enneagram is one of the many personality profiling systems in today's world. However, its origin remains relatively unclear. There are groups of people who believe that Enneagram comes from The X or XI centuries among the Sufi, which is a mystical sect of Islam. There are others who believe that Enneagram existed much earlier, in 2500 BC in Babylon, in today's Middle East.

Regardless of when the Enneagram was created, it still remains a very accurate tool to profile people today, simply because human nature is in all these years hasn't really changed.

The Enneagram is also one of the few dynamic profiling systems in circulation. Instead of boxing people describes how the person will behave when feeling good or under stress, and shows how a man should grow up to achieve his potential in life.

In total, there are nine basic personality types, and these personalities are described using numbers, instead of words. The Reason for using numbers is to keep things neutral. Words have a tendency to create meaning in our minds, and we might unknowingly become biased towards certain types because of cultural or societal influence.

Therefore, the nine types are denoted by numbers from one to nine and the numbers bear similar weights, which means that they have a greater number of figures, does not entail that it is better or worse.

You will encounter different and sequential teachings that use different words to describe types. Remember that descriptions are really for illustrative purposes and are designed to give you a better understanding of the type. Different sources use different words to describe each species, so don't be confused about it.

Each personality type has nine levels of health, from the healthiest to level one, the most unhealthy to level nine. So, if you calculate all possible combinations using the wings and lines, as well as health levels, you look at potentially four hundred and eight six variations of personality types.

With so many possible combinations, how exactly do you profile someone? Unlike many of the other personality profiles that require the use of surveys or questionnaires, you can actually profile somebody with the Enneagram simply for observation.

Of course, the length of your observation will definitely affect the accuracy of your profiling. Although we are indeed a single basic type, every one of us will respond according to different situations and environments in which we find ourselves. Therefore, it is not surprising that we will show the characteristics of nine types of personality throughout our life. So the best time to observe is over their time, or in the most natural state.

You can always use the questionnaire to profile someone or confirm your comments. However, with time and practice, you will realize that you can do without a questionnaire. It would give you a huge boost to improve your interpersonal communication skills and definitely adds more value to you as an effective communicator.

Enneagram and Your Inner Motivation

Reformer, assistant, successful, individualist, Observer, loyalist, passionate, challenger and peacemaker.

Welcome to the new perspective of personality! A simple, but profound system of types of human personality, the Enneagram can help you to find what truly leads you and all the other persons that you know in your life-and how to make the most of these insights.

You can get a lot from knowing your type and others around you, it's just, let's say... Find out "what color your personality has". With Enneagram, you can really have a vision in yourself and find out what really motivates you in the center. Rediscover your passion.

Let's think about it... That job feels a little more tortured, and you're going through your days like a zombie? Wake up, go to work, come home late and tired, maybe grumpy-flop on the bed, rinse and repeat. Well, maybe the answer is simple: if your work fails to meet your internal motivation, it will never be very satisfying for you. You're just going through the movements.

Or, if the work is fantastic, and you just want to better understand people, like your crush or that quiet girl that won't leave a corner, or even that guy boring you will not stop to boast about, the Enneagram can be of great benefit to look at things from their point of view. You can learn how to get along with specific types of people, compatibility with them, and also what they think about you. Find what makes them happy.

And I promise it'll be as much fun as finding out what color your personality is, if not more.

Here is a brief overview of Nine personality types:

Reformer / Perfectionist

Reformers live by high standards, because they always try to do everything right and do everything right. They are the most reliable people you have ever met, righteous and honest, who adhere firmly to principles and ethics. Always realistic and reasonable, they strive for the ideal-but they are far from being an inactive Dreamer. In life, perfectionists want to avoid anger and mistakes.

Assistant

Everyone likes to receive, appreciate and need - helpers make it the essence of life. They try to achieve this by projecting a positive and warm presence and trying to take care of the needs of the people around them. As a result, people are especially happy when they are nearby. It helps to avoid journalists in need.

Result

Drive pupils to succeed and be productive and everything revolves around these goals. Always confident, they are everything they seem and tend to be role models that inspire others. Those who succeed abhor and do their best to avoid it.

Individualist

Individualists live on the border between real life and fantastic life. It seems to almost disappear in the Middle, always comparing what they actually have and what they would like to have (but most of all they can't). Individualists are forced to find the true meaning of life, discover yourself, look for things that they want in life, and not be just another face. They want to be special because in reality these people are special... And you know better.

Observer

Observers like to monitor their various interests and thoughts on their own. They are motivated by a deep need to know and understand everything and be self-sufficient. Observers wish for themselves, and only for themselves, not others, to control them, which makes them the last independent individuals. They try to avoid looking stupid or incompetent.

The Loyalist

Loyalists usually seek a sense of security. Loyalists come in many flavors, from withdrawn and inflexible, bold and conflicting. There are two types of six: phobia and contra phobia. The first looks scary and seeks consent. He fights with his fear, he seems fearless and open. Both focus on treating fear.

Enthusiast

If you don't know the age limit, always elastic, always active and always busy, most likely you seven-passionate. Fans are motivated by the need to be happy and have fun, be beneficial to the world and eliminate pain and suffering.

The Challenger

The first word that comes to mind to describe people of this type, should be "strong", because the challengers seek to be strong and self-reliant. They want to avoid being considered weak... and people who somehow think they are would soon get what comes out of them anyway.

Peacemaker

Peacekeepers are simply made adaptable and neutral, because they have a deep need to maintain peace and connect with others and avoid conflicts.

Since they are so adaptable, they are significantly affected by the other eight types that surround them. Consequently, there is a wide variety of peace workers, from people with a strong and independent nature and kind personality.

So, what do you think you are?

If you are interested to learn more, including:

personality test-short and practical, or long and scientifically valid;

examples of all kinds in real life;

Discover the three main motivations of self-image, fear and anger.

Voice and Enneagram

Voice and Enneagram

Our voice is much more than a communication tool. The breath of the air flowing into your body, takes your unique thoughts, feelings and emotions, and when they appear again, it is filled with your essence.

There is no better way to understand a person by the way he uses his voice:

* The voice to circulate freely or is it braked?

* Is the voice tense or relaxed?

* Is the voice strong and rooted or is it too light?

* Does the voice use the breath economically or greedily?

* Full voice or lack of feelings and emotions?

The shadows of our voice reflect our physical, mental and emotional state, constantly emit frequencies and vibrations that indicate what and how we think and feel, beyond our words. He never lies, no matter how hard we try to hide our voice.

This unique ability of our voice resonates with the basic Enneagram, 9 spiritual passions that dominate our thoughts, feelings and emotions. Each type has its own voice model that reflects the forces and corresponds to this type of specific experience. Listening to your voice helps you identify what you're going through, what's holding you back and what blind spots you missed.

The voice is physical. It arises from vibrations on the vocal cords, powered by breathing, amplified cavities in the body and understandable use of shock absorbers. A voice shift is often easier and faster than a change in mind.

A quick example. People tried to tell each other how often to keep their calm in a situation of nervousness, stress and anger. Not much worked until they begin to take the right breath and support their voice with the breath, their trembling voice begins to take control.

Free your voice, free your mind. Reveal the voice that comes out of your heart, release the feelings and emotions that you have retained. Fully resonate your voice, experience transformations in the way you express and speak for yourself.

The Enneagram As a Master Tool for Transformation

Enneagram is an ancient instrument, of uncertain origin, said to have been introduced truth, some genes like. Also called Sufis numbers is like chess and other amazing design things that have always been around.

The Enneagram is an overview of the nine basic personality types; it shows the advantages and limitations of any intelligent being born on this planet.

The outline of Nine personality types, with a modern interpretation is as follows.

1. Perfectionist, number one is a very disciplined person, he wants the best quality at all costs. They make great bad characters in films, because they are very indifferent to human suffering, they are the perfect Inquisitor.

2. Server, also known as an assistant, or Saint. Usually these are very service-oriented people who help everyone. Sometimes they become intrusive manipulators who want others to do what they want, because they think this is the only good and a good way to do it in the universe. The classic is a beggar screaming at people.

3. Chameleon, also known as a climber. The guy is handsome and talented, but his kindness is barely noticeable. You can see how they change before your eyes and turn against you when a crisis occurs. No one can believe that they are false personalities, because they build a beautiful smile and look good, when in fact they are somehow separated from their true feelings.

4. Extra sensitive is an artist as a personality. A tendency to depression and envy about what others have done with their lives. Some suicidal tendencies are possible because he is aware of his own impulses while feeling guilty. To others, it may seem that such

a person exaggerates in his emotional fears about the reactions of other peoples.

5. Paranoid Nerd. The guy is very intellectual, but at the same time he is distracted. He sees a logical connection in everything. He always wants to know the explanation of the phenomena that occur everywhere. He can be paranoid and build conspiracy theories and treat all drugs. He likes recognition for his brilliant mind and also wants to find a way to adapt to the word, which they consider scary.

6. The devil is the defender. It can be a faithful Apprentice or a bad enemy of scandalous gossip. Inside, he has a lot of tension that relieves him by finding the worst possible interpretation of the behavior of others and telling everyone what his twisted mind thinks. He may seem like an indifferent bastard, but he is a very conscientious worker and a masochistic character.

7. Manic. Peter Pan's guy. they never grow up. He's still an immature child. He screams and fights for

things and objects that he needs so much that it's even scary. It can be food, video games, a ticket to the theater, call him. He is selfish and does not bother too often to share goods evenly.

8. A tyrannical dictator. He could also be a great boss or boss. He has a very powerful personality, always rooted in the final sum. When he is unbalanced, he can act as a mafia leader and threaten anyone who does not fulfill his desires. On the other hand, he could be a real hero and a philanthropist.

9. Nine is the most unavailable person on the planet. A peacemaker, an alienated unconscious person who lives in endless silent disconnection. He or she can go to a party with you and completely forget that you are there. Sometimes they have alarm clocks like, oh my God, but you've been here all this time!

The Enneagram is actually the main tool for transformation uses group dynamics trainers to create a transformation exercise, touching all aspects of pool restrictions on human shadow, with the intention of overcoming it. He creates the greatest discoveries in the transformations of the Master of Shadows, and these are very serious studies.

Using the Enneagram to Develop Mindfulness and Your Self Observer

The Enneagram-a personality typing system that breaks the human selfish personality into 9 different types - can be used as a very accurate tool, how to develop your own Observer. A self-Observer is a subject beyond your ego-sometimes described as "consciousness" - in you who watches you do what you do.

It's like discovering more intelligence in itself. Instead of being a conspirator, planner, critic and judge; this "other spirit" is one who conceptualizes, appreciates art, sees the global image and understands God.

A short exercise can help you discover this side of you.

Close your eyes for a second and focus on your breathing. Settle down. So focus on your stomach. Watch how your stomach swells and tightens when breathing. Now move your consciousness from your feet. Then move your consciousness to any place where there are tensions in your body and breathe in that place. You can feel it expanding and relaxing. Now transfer your consciousness to your emotions.

How are you feeling? Are you excited? Shaken? Anxious?? Are you fired, feeding or feeling depressed? Notice how you feel.

Now focus on what you hear no noise, no matter how small it is in your environment. Take two more breaths and open your eyes.

As you have moved through this exercise, your consciousness has gone from breathing to stomach on legs to your emotions and eventually wherever you feel the tension.

But like you did, there was another part of you that knew where your attention was. How else did you know where to get your attention? Have you been a part of me who knew where your attention is and who could change your consciousness in other places.

Or look at you in the Mirror, who is the one who looks at your reflection when you look?

This is your inner Observer.

He's always been there, whether you know it or not, and you can train him to watch you do what you do. This inner Observer watches us dance and realize ourselves.

And Enneagram, when used effectively, is designed to help your inner observer look at you more subtly. It can increase your self-awareness, at an accelerated pace.

Instead of a whiteboard, it's like having a map to help you understand your personal landscape-the way you see the world-in more detail. This is the difference between falling into a new country blind against Reading and getting books and tourist maps before leaving.

An inner observer can often feel as if he is behind you or above you, watching you dance. When you become competent in its use, you will be able to separate yourself from the thoughts circulating in your mind, and therefore from your reactivity to them. You have the choice to engage in thought-or let it pass.

Our selfish mind - our unconscious self-esteem - is absolutely determined to be in the driver's seat. Your mind would make you think it was you. But in fact, your mind is just another part of you - like your heart and body. Its main purpose is to preserve, so it will do everything in its power to stay in the driver's seat. And because he knows you intimately, he spews up all the stuff in the book so he doesn't realize your conscience.

It would make you think that these are your emotional reactions, that you are the fear that you feel, that you are the pain that you feel ... that you are thoughts that move in our minds. In fact, there is something behind it-The Observer.

As we begin to observe and separate from their reactions, thoughts, feelings, emotions and sensations, begins to emerge authentic self, often called the "conscious"self.

When this happens, we present ourselves in a world with greater presence and intention. We will connect with the source, God, Infinity-whatever you choose to call it. It comes through us. Some have described it as a spirit with human experience.

As our self-awareness grows, we begin to look for a diminishing reaction. You can actually witness thoughts of anger, sadness, etc. I come thanks to you. And yet you did not hold it. It is thanks to this observation that we can see our reaction.

Enneagram can help you in this process.

Enneagram coach Ben Saltzman describes an example in his life. He said, "I'm type 7, and I know that when I'm on the Type, I have an inner departure from pain, pain and suffering. There's something in me that doesn't want to be present."

"When I started watching it, I saw it perform in the movie. When the painful moment came, I began to turn my thinking into a wonderful seminar that I am about to do next week."

"My observer saw me doing it and I realized I was jumping out of my heart and into my head. I don't have this experience of pain and suffering. Email. Instead, I moved to a nice and pleasant future alternative, which is where Type 7 Love."

He says that the self-awareness provided by Enneagram helped him become more comfortable with pain and suffering. And that, in turn, makes him a better coach. He said: "If you want to do a deep job with your customers, it's important to go with them.

We often go with customers to places where it hurts, or where there is pain and fear. If I can't leave them a seat because I feel uncomfortable and want to leave the room, they'll want to leave. You don't need it.

Each of us has its own development path and Enneagram can provide a roadmap for this trip. It allows you to see your "stuff", clean and opens the door, internal changes that create lasting and transformational changes in our lives. As we work with this system, the world reacts and opens up.

This may sound paradoxical, but the way we use our self-observer to examine how our type, the Enneagram plays in the United States, becomes a portal to get out of the type we're stuck with. It helps us see our reactions in our lives. We enter the place of freedom.

Often you have to start thinking about the day and think " how my type of spin today? What's going on? What happened?"

For a guy 7 like Ben who can play around with questions like "when did I go through hard times or boredom? When do I get away from the pain and suffering and get it in my head?"

You may find that you made a game of your type - you backed away instead of pushing forward, diverted your attention, instead of focusing, or I nervously playful, when a serious firm was appropriate. And you can say that you turned away, turned away turned away and you were impressed, and this is not what you want. But the fundamental thing is that you have witnessed yourself, practiced self-denial.

And then-in what will look like a magical moment - you will be surprised that you are doing it right now, right now. This is the moment when the true gift of self-control comes ... you can make a different choice.

Often the entrance to this moment requires "breathing" to open the space to find out what is true for you at this moment. This may require you to apply and know what you really want to do or how you really want to react.

Sometimes it's as simple as saying, "No, I don't want to do more, I prefer to do it."At other times, it may seem complicated. But always remember that once you make your observers to now, taken, you have a gift to be able to make new choices-right now.

How can you train and develop your observer?

One way is breathing exercises that will slow down your thoughts. You can do this by realizing your breath and counting when you breathe. Breathe when you count to seven. Hold. Then exhale seven more times.

Meditation is one of the best ways to calm your mind and develop your observers. You will probably go through what Buddhists call "monkey Spirit"; your mind will do anything but try to become. Try to keep your attention on your breathing - "inhale, exhale ... inhale, exhale."

And stay with him. It may take some time, but suddenly you find yourself in a conscious state, you look at your " mental mind "separately from your "conscious mind", almost like another appendix like a hand, foot or leg. It's an amazing experience when it happens. You see hovering thoughts as you look at the images through the motion screen.

Other people think that nature is a great place to calm their minds. Only observing how nature develops in all its different ways helps to calm the mind. As well as gardening, fishing and yoga. For me, one of my favorite ways to repeat aerobic exercises, such as jogging, cross-country skiing or rowing.

Personal Growth Through the Enneagram

Have you ever spent hours on a puzzle to realize that a key piece is missing? Your first answer is probably: "you can't lose. It must be somewhere over there."You will take in return every piece available. Look under the table and on the floor. Slide your fingers through the finished parts of the puzzle, hoping that your fingers will see something that your eyes have overlooked.

You can leave the Puzzle here, which is the missing piece. It is more difficult to walk with the hope that your life will merge into a meaningful whole. The Enneagram is a system of reasoning about human personality and motivation, which helps people understand the patterns in their own lives and the lives of the people around them. Many people use Enneagram to discover the piece they feared was missing.

Based on a combination of ancient wisdom and modern social science, The Enneagram is a model that describes the models that people generally use to motivate themselves, interact with others and cope with threats or obstacles. At the heart of the system is the recognition that the strategies that work best for us eventually become errors that make us vulnerable. We do not always have strengths and weaknesses: sometimes the same quality is both strength and weakness.

It's one thing to overcome your mistakes. Another thing is to overcome your strengths. The Enneagram describes from the point of view of what you want most, what you fear most, and what you will probably have to do to get the results you want. It is dynamic in the way humans are dynamic; The Enneagram describes how we change when we feel confident or stressed and how we move each other in different contexts. A circle with nine points, Enneagram describes us all as part of a whole, a human family in which we are all connected and connected.

A lot of information about Enneagram is available online and in libraries. There are many tests you can do that will begin on how to understand your Enneagram type. In the field of Enneagram studies, tests are only tips: they show the starting point, not the conclusion. There is no substitute for talking about your samples with other Enneagram students. In addition to identifying yourself through your family and professional relationships, you can better identify yourself in the Enneagram tradition from the opinions of others about the models you have experienced.

Even a weekend course with good help allows you to see more of yourself and see in others. Start identifying new pieces of your personal puzzle and see how others build a completely different puzzle in your life. You will have a new perspective to promote a new quality in understanding yourself and your relationships with others.

If you ever feel like missing a key part of your personal puzzle, consider learning more about Enneagram. You will create a new sense of how the patterns of your life are repeated and combined with the creation of a single set. You will develop a new understanding of patterns in the behavior of others. Sow seeds for renewed enthusiasm and satisfaction in building and maintaining relationships.

Learn more about Enneagram. Discover the patterns of your personal puzzles-and find all the necessary pieces.

Enhancing Relationships With the Enneagram

What difference would it make to your life if your relationships, at home and at work, were based on mutual understanding and respect, where you inspire each other to be your best and enjoy the differences between you? The Enneagram is a powerful and still surprisingly little known approach to understanding our personality type and that of the people we are close to, and it helps us to create and enjoy wonderfully fulfilling, happy relationships that just get better over time.

With insights from the Enneagram, we can maximize the potential for fun, connections, love, and growth in our relationships, rather than endure problems based on misunderstandings.

How does it work then, I can hear you asking? Well, first you need to understand what type you are and identify what areas of development you have within your type---and by the way, it's much easier to work on your development when you have specific, individual areas to look at, rather than a generic, one size fits all self-help approach.

What is Your Enneagram Type?

There are 9 basic personality types, each of which has one of three essential frameworks through which they view and filter the world: analytic, where we have an intellectual first response; emotional, where our first response is a feeling one; and instinctive, where we first have a gut reaction to a situation. Just knowing which of these 3 frameworks is primary, immediately gives us a short-cut to deeper understanding.

Type 1: The Reformer, idealistic and perfectionist

Type 2: The Helper, motivated by the need to be valued

Type 3: The Achiever, ambitious and driven

Type 4: The Individualist, romantic and artistic

Type 5: The Thinker, analytical and detached

Type 6: The Loyalist, motivated by the need for security

Type 7: The Adventurer, enthusiastic and fun-loving

Type 8: The Challenger, assertive and direct

Type 9: The Peacemaker, mediating and non-confrontational

It's Dynamic, Not Static

Unlike most other personality testing you might have done in the past, the Enneagram does not simply put you in a box or category, but instead shows you how to develop to become the best version of your personality type.

Each of the 9 types is much more complex than the simple description above might apply, and each type will come across differently depending on where they are on the spectrum of emotional health.

Compatibility?

You are probably wondering at this point whether certain types are more compatible than others. The answer is yes and no...Yes, because some types find it easier to understand and connect with each other, and no, because it depends ultimately on the level of development and self-awareness of each type. A very healthy one, for example, can get along beautifully with a similarly healthy person of any type, whereas an unhealthy two, for example, might find type 9 with its tendency to withdraw unbearably frustrating emotionally.

So What Can The Enneagram Do To Help You Strengthen Your Relationships?

It Helps People Communicate

By helping us be lucidly conscious of who and how we are in relationships, what our framework of expectations is, what brings out the best (and the worst) in us, we understand what we need from the other person, and equally what can trigger a negative spiral.

For example, if you're dealing with a heart-centred and aesthetic type Four, you wouldn't approach them initially in an analytical and impersonal way.

It Gives You a Specific Approach and Plan For Maximising Your Relationships

You can maximize harmony and trust by understanding the enneagram type of your friend, and create a clear plan for allowing the relationship to deliver its potential.

It Helps You Enjoy Your Relationships More

It Helps You Avoid and Resolve Conflict

Each type has a specific pattern in how it deals with conflict, and understanding this pattern allows you to resolve any tension quickly and concentrate on positive solutions instead. Some types deal with conflict by immediately looking for a positive, best-case scenario approach for solutions, whereas others have an emotionally intense response that needs to be understood, and others go into analytical mode. And of course we need all three approaches to resolve conflict successfully.

Just for fun, here are some examples of famous Enneagram couples. Can you see the potential patterns from the brief introduction I've just given you?   Six and Four: Princess Diana and Prince Charles Seven and Four: Rhett Butler and Scarlett O' Hara Eight and Two: J.R. Ewing and Sue Ellen in Dallas Nine and One: Bill and Hillary Clinton

I use the Enneagram as a fundamental part of my coaching approach with clients, and regularly get feedback that the new understanding they have has transformed a difficult relationship at work into one of mutual support and respect, or turned a stressful pattern of conflict in a personal relationship into a new pattern of mutual understanding and renewed connection. Whether used as the framework for an executive coaching workshop on team development, or used in life coaching for personal development, the Enneagram always gets rave reviews from my clients.

Having conscious awareness of our own way of seeing the world and that of the people we are close to, gives us the tool kit to create the positive, happy relationships we want, as well as allowing relationships to be part of our spiritual and emotional journey of development towards our best self.

Kind reader,

Thank you very much. I hope you enjoyed the book.

Can I ask you a big favor?

I would be grateful if you would please take a few minutes to leave me a gold star on Amazon.

Thank you again for your support.

Rebecca Hood